Sing Me, Goddess

W. W. CRUICKSHANK

1912- 2003
(SPS 1947 – 1973)

Achilles, from an amphora in the Vatican by the
'Achilles Painter' (about 440 B.C.). Photo: Alinari

SING ME, GODDESS

being
the First Recitation
of Homer's Iliad
translated
by

M. L. West

DUCKWORTH

First published in 1971 by
Gerald Duckworth & Co. Ltd.
3 Henrietta Street, London, WC2

ISBN 0 7156 0595 X

Printed in Great Britain by
Western Printing Services Ltd, Bristol

INTRODUCTION

THE Greeks of the early classical period, down to
the end of the sixth century B.C., depended for
their knowledge of the past on heroic poetry more
than anything else. They had no written records of
any kind that went back earlier than the eighth
century, when they learned an alphabet from the
Phoenicians, and no one had yet attempted to make
a history out of what little there was. In epic
poetry, on the other hand, they possessed a wealth
of stories from much earlier times: stories of a
heroic age when men were closer to the gods, often
fathered by them; lordly men and strong and proud,
feasting daily on meat from inexhaustible herds,
rich in gold and silver, but living above all for
glory and honour. Many were the poems about
this age that the trained minstrels sang or recited to
the accompaniment of the lyre in the mansions of
the wealthy, in the market-place, and at public
games and festivals.

Their performances meant livelihood for them,
entertainment and instruction for their audiences,
and for a long time it was being heard rather than
being read that made these poems widely known.
Some of them existed in writing, and in time the
minstrels came to depend entirely on the written ver-

sions. But the style was formed under conditions like those in which popular heroic poetry has been composed in more recent times in Yugoslavia, Russia and elsewhere. Each performer learns the traditional stories from his older contemporaries, and a traditional style for telling them. He does not necessarily set out to add anything original; but it is easier for him to re-tell the tale in verses of his own, each time he recites, than to reproduce what he has heard word for word. In this way memories of real historical events and of the cultural conditions of past ages can be handed down over many centuries, though they become distorted and unreliable in detail, and receive many a fictional embellishment. Greek epic bears the characteristic marks of this type of oral tradition. Its narrative is built up according to certain typical principles which help the poet to organize his material and know what to describe next. Its language is full of formulaic phrases handed down from one poet to another and repeated as often as convenient; it shows little desire for variety or novelty of expression, and there are many archaisms of vocabulary and grammar. Archaeology confirms that it enshrines genuine memories of the second millennium B.C., preserved through centuries in which the Greeks were ignorant of writing. We know today that the towns remembered in epic as being rich and powerful in the heroic age actually were so in the Mycenaean period, and in most cases never again. Among the many famous deeds associated with those towns, the greatest and most famous was the sack of Troy after ten years of war; later chroniclers calculated that this happened a little before or after 1200 B.C. We know today that Troy existed, and that it really was destroyed by an enemy in the thirteenth century. However, we must not exaggerate the dependability of the tradition. Apart from the basic fact that Troy fell, it is unsafe to treat the events or personalities described in the epics about the Trojan War as historical. Some of them may be, but others will have been imported from other stories or invented in the long course of the tradition. The scale of the Greek expedition has certainly been grossly exaggerated.

The *Iliad* and *Odyssey* are the only two of those poems that have come down to us. They were by the common consent of antiquity the greatest of them; and the *Iliad* is the greater of the two. The *Odyssey* is a charming and in parts a stirring poem: the *Iliad* is a sublime poem. Its construction is not faultless, and the generous stretches of battle narrative may fail to grip the modern reader who has never seen and is too lazy to imagine such a thing as a *spear* going through a *man*. But the drama of the central characters reveals an artist with quite exceptional depths of humanity. Their relationships to one another are founded on clear-cut basic emotions—love, grief, fear, hate, resentment, compassion—arising in natural response to drastic events, with no unheroic complexity of character to detract from their intensity. Whoever is unmoved by the *Iliad* ought seriously to investigate whether he has a heart.

Ten years have passed since the abduction oı Helen from the palace of Menelaus, and the war is now nearing its end. The Greeks, who in Homer are usually called Achaeans, sometimes Danaans or Argives, are encamped by the Dardanelles, living in their ships, which are drawn up on the beach, and in wooden cabins. Troy, also called Ilios, lies on a hill a few miles inland, on the other side of the broad plain that is the scene of battle. The commander-in-chief of the Achaeans is the king of Mycenae, Agamemnon, sometimes called Atri-des or son of Atreus; Menelaus is his brother. Troy is ruled by the old king Priam, but it is on one of his sons, Hector, that the city's hopes of salvation principally rest. The *Iliad* is the story of the death of Hector at the merciless hands of Achilles. Before a major hero is killed, his importance is regularly emphasized by giving him a period of particular success in battle. In order for Hector to be shown in this role, the one man capable of killing him must be otherwise occupied, and for the whole earlier part of the *Iliad* Achilles stays out of the fighting, in consequence of a quarrel with Agame-mnon. This is the Anger of Achilles that Homer asks to hear from his goddess the Muse in the first line of the poem. It is only when Achilles' great friend Patroclus is killed by Hector that he is moved to return to the field, to take vengeance on the perpetrator of the deed.

The ancients divided the *Iliad* into twenty-four *rhapsodiai*, 'recitations'. There was an obvious place for at least one of these divisions to be marked, for the first 611 lines of the poem form a relatively self-contained introduction to the whole, covering the events preceding the first day on which the Greeks go out to fight without Achilles. It tells how Achilles and Agamemnon came to quarrel, and how Zeus the king of heaven then determined that Agamemnon's forces should have the worst of the fighting until such time as Achilles was restored to full honour. It is a most skilful and assured composition. The quarrel itself—no easy thing to dramatize convincingly—is masterly: Homer has the gift of throwing himself into each of his characters, feeling their feelings and speaking with their voices, and the way in which he makes the two proud men provoke each other further with each reply could not be bettered. Some of the other participants who perhaps need more introduction on their first appearance, like Calchas and Nestor, are given it. We also meet most of the gods and goddesses who will play significant parts in the narrative: Zeus the Olympian father, son of Kronos, who wields the thunderbolt and imposes his will on the rest; Hera, his scolding wife, who sometimes tries to interfere with his plans, but never with full understanding or lasting effect; Phoebus Apollo the far-shooter, his son by Leto, a god of particular power in the land about Troy; Pallas Athena, who deals with the Greek heroes on personal terms and stands by them in battle; Hephaestus, the lame, good-humoured craftsman of the gods; and Thetis the sea-nymph, daughter of the Old Man of the Sea, and mother of Achilles. Many memorable passages of description, too, help to qualify this first recitation as a worthy sample for those who are not yet acquainted with the whole.

A translator should aim to reproduce the spirit and manner of the original no less faithfully than he renders the words. Few of the versions of Homer that have been served upon the public in recent years, and apparently received with much acclaim, fulfil this requirement. Flavourless, uncertain prose, prose interspersed with jingly verse, prose divided up as if it were itself verse, will not do, however lively or contemporary it may be. Homer is poetry, rhythmical poetry, stylistically remote from any prose ever written. His Greek was not, even to his original audience, contemporary or colloquial: it was archaic and elevated. If modern English poetry has turned its back on archaism and elevation, and for that matter rhythm, the translator must look elsewhere for models. After all, he is not trying to contribute to modern English poetry, he is trying to give an idea of what early Greek poetry was like.

The idea that the metre of the *Kalevala* might be the best medium for translating Homer lodged in my mind several years before I started doing it. Personally, I find ordinary blank verse, and long lines generally, wearisome to read in any quantity; the short verse of the *Kalevala,* with its trochaic rhythm, has a rapidity that leads one on painlessly. It also has the advantage of being a metre familar to English readers in association with formulaic language, if not from the *Kalevala,* from Longfellow's imitation, *Hiawatha.* I have found it a manageable instrument, and good friends have encouraged me to think that the result is worth exhibiting in public.

April 1971   M. L. W.

SING me, goddess, of the anger
of Achilles, son of Peleus,
bane that brought to the Achaeans
countless woe, and hurled to Hades
countless mighty hero spirits,
left to dogs and birds their carrion,
and the will of Zeus accomplished.
Sing from when they first made quarrel,
Agamemnon, king of peoples,
and the noble-born Achilles.

Which god set them at a quarrel?
Zeus' and Leto's son, in anger
at the king, and plagued the army,
and the warrior hordes were dying:
for his priest Atrides slighted,
Chryses, when to the Achaeans
he brought ransom for his daughter,
brought them boundless compensation,
held the wreaths of lord Apollo
on his golden staff, and begged them,
chiefly begged the sons of Atreus,
twin arrayers of the war-horde:
'Sons of Atreus, and Achaeans,
may the gods upon Olympus
grant you sack of Priam's city,

13

and returning home in safety:
but take ransom for my daughter,
and accept my compensation,
fearing Zeus' son, lord Apollo.'

Then the others all consented,
Serve the priest, said the Achaeans,
and accept his compensation.
But Atrides Agamemnon
sent him roughly on his business,
and in harsh words gave him counsel:
'No more, old man, let me find you
by the warships, now or ever,
or your staff may not avail you
and the wreaths of lord Apollo.
Her I will not ransom, sooner
will she grow old in my palace,
far in Argos from her homeland,
at the loom and at my pillow.
Now begone, do not provoke me,
if you would return in safety.'

Then in fear the old man yielded,
said no word but went in silence
up the beach beside the breakers.
Many prayers from there he uttered
to Apollo, son of Leto:
'Hear me, god with bow of silver,
lord of Chryse, lord of Killa,
lord of Tenedos, great Smintheus!
Have I never decked your temple?
Have I never burnt fat thighbones,

burnt you bones of goats and oxen?
Grant my prayer then: for my weeping
let the army of the Danaans
pay the price upon thy arrows.'

And Apollo heard his praying,
from Olympus came in anger
with his bow upon his shoulder,
and the arrows in the quiver
rattled as he rose in anger.
Like the night he came and settled
near the ships, and shot an arrow,
and the silver bow rang deadly.
First the dogs and mules he worked at,
then at men his shafts directed.

Every day the pyres were burning;
nine days long the god's compulsion
visited the warrior army.
On the tenth day swift Achilles
called the war-host to assembly;
white-armed Hera set him to it,
troubled at the Danaans dying.
When the war-host was assembled,
he stood forward and addressed them:
'Son of Atreus, now I see us
turning back to journey homeward,
if we do not die yet sooner;
war and plague together break us.
Let us ask a seer for counsel,
priest of god, or dream-expounder:
even dreams show Zeus's purpose.

He could tell us of the reason
for this anger of Apollo's,
whether he is discontented
with our vows or sacrificing,
whether sheep's or goat's fat burning
would appease him and persuade him
to protect us from destruction.'
After speaking he was seated.

Then did Calchas, son of Thestor,
best of augurs, stand before them,
he who knew what is and will be
and whatever was aforetime.
He the ships of the Achaeans
brought to Ilios by his wisdom
that he had from lord Apollo.
Wishing well he spoke among them:
'Great Achilles, whom Zeus favours,
you would have me tell the anger
of Apollo the far-shooter.
I will speak, but you shall promise,
say on oath you will support me
with your words and with your body,
for I fear that I shall anger
one whose power is great in Argos,
and Achaeans all obey him.
Mightier is a king in quarrel
than a man of lesser virtue:
he may swallow down his ire
on the day, but still it rankles
in his heart and seeks fulfilment.

Say then if you will protect me.'
    Swift Achilles spoke in answer:
'If you know God's will, reveal it,
fear not; for by great Apollo—
whom you pray to for the Danaans,
Calchas, and God's will discover—
while I live beneath this heaven
none shall raise his hand against you
of the Danaans by the warships,
no, not even Agamemnon,
he who now of the Achaeans
claims to have the highest standing.'
    Then the good seer spoke more boldly:
'He is neither discontented
with our vows nor sacrificing;
but his priest Atrides slighted,
and his daughter would not ransom,
nor accept his compensation.
Therefore has the god far-shooting
sent us woe, and will send longer:
he will not fend off destruction
from the Danaans till they render
that fair maiden to her father,
without fee or compensation,
and a sacrifice of oxen
consecrate and send to Chryse.
That would please him and persuade him.'
After speaking he was seated.
    Then Atrides Agamemnon,
emperor hero, stood before them,

17

sore, his black lungs big with anger,
and his eyes like flashing fire.
Boding ill he spoke to Calchas:
'Prophet that you are of evil,
words of cheer you never bring me.
You like evil prophesyings,
fair prediction have you never
uttered or fulfilled among us.
Now you make your divination
and you say before the Danaans
that the god far-shooting sends them
woe because for Chryses' daughter
I would take no compensation.
I will have her in my palace;
greatly I prefer her even
to my lady Clytemnestra.
She is no less fair of figure,
no less sensible or skilful.
Yet I'll yield her, if it must be;
'tis my mind to save the war-host,
not to see it perish wholly.
Now another trophy find me,
lest I be alone untrophied
of the Argives—'tis not fitting:
all your eyes do see it plainly,
that my trophy is departing.'
    Swift Achilles spoke in answer:
'Agamemnon, king most glorious,
and of all most avaricious,
how then shall the proud Achaeans

18

render you another trophy?
We can see no mass of booty
lying still for distribution.
What we had from sacking townships
is divided, 'tis not fitting
that the host again collect it.
Yield the girl, the god appeasing:
the Achaeans shall repay you
threefold, fourfold, if Zeus grants us
sack of Troy's strong-wallèd city.'

   Great Atrides spoke in answer:
'Brave Achilles, like the immortals,
do not try so to deceive me;
you will not outwit or win me.
Do you want to keep your trophy,
but to have me sit without one,
so you bid me yield the maiden?
If indeed the proud Achaeans
will provide another trophy,
like in worth, to my heart's measure,
good; but if they will not give one,
I myself will go and take one,
yours, or Aias', or Odysseus',
and the man that I do visit
shall be angry at my taking.
That we may consider later:
now we must take down a black ship
to the sea, and muster rowers,
and a sacrifice of oxen
put aboard, and fair Chryseis.

And let someone be commander,
lord Idomeneus, or Aias,
or Odysseus, or yourself then,
son of Peleus most exceeding,
so that you by sacrificing
may appease Apollo for us.'
    Swift Achilles answered frowning:
'So! Advantage is your liking,
brazenness your shoulders' mantle.
How should one of the Achaeans
willingly obey your bidding,
go a journey, or do battle?
I came not to fight in battles
on account of Trojan spearmen,
for I have no quarrel with them.
They have never stolen from me
cows or horses, they have never
harmed my crops in fertile Phthia:
great the distance that divides us,
sounding sea and shadowed mountains.
You, o brazen one, did bring us
for your joy, that Menelaus
and your shameless self might levy
restitution from the Trojans:
this you mind not and regard not.
Now you bid to take my trophy,
which to win I laboured greatly,
and the Achaeans gave it to me.
Never do I get a trophy
great as yours, when the Achaeans

sack a township of the Trojans.
My hands most in furious battle
work, but at a distribution
yours is much the greater trophy;
I go off with but a small one,
small and precious, to my vessels,
weary as I am of fighting.
Now I will return to Phthia:
better far to take my beaked ships
homeward, for I do not fancy
staying here, deprived of honour,
drawing you your wealth and riches.'

    Answered him king Agamemnon:
'Fly, if so your spirit urges.
I beseech you not, for my sake
here to dally; I have others
who will give my due of honour,
chiefly Zeus the counsel-maker.
Most of all the kings I loathe you;
you like quarrels, war, and fighting.
If you're strong, 'tis God's bestowing.
Go home with your ships and comrades,
over Myrmidons be monarch.
I care nothing for your anger;
and I give you now this warning:
Phoebus claims Chryseis from me;
her then with my ships and comrades
will I render; but for my part
I will come for fair Briseis,
take your trophy from your cabin,

teach you how I rank above you,
and another man shall tremble
to oppose me as my equal.'
   At his words the son of Peleus
suffered anguish; in his rough breast
did the heart two counsels ponder,
whether to draw forth the sharp sword
from his thigh, to rouse the men up,
and to slay the son of Atreus,
or to check his angry spirit.
Thus he pondered, mind and spirit,
grasped the great sword in his scabbard,
when Athena came from heaven:
white-armed Hera sent her thither,
troubled for her two dear warriors.
She behind the son of Peleus
stood and took him by his brown hair;
none but he alone might see her.
Then Achilles turned, astonished,
straightway recognized Athena—
dreadful were her eyes a-gleaming—
and in wingèd words addressed her.
'Child of Zeus that bears the aegis,
have you come to see the insults
of Atrides Agamemnon?
Let me tell you this prediction:
by his arrogant demeanour
he is like to leave his spirit.'
   Answered him pale-eyed Athena:
'I have come to check your temper,

if it please you, down from heaven:
white-armed Hera sent me hither,
troubled for her two dear warriors.
Come, your enmity abandon;
from your grasp the sword relinquish,
and in words rebuke and warn him.
For I tell you this prediction:
thrice increased fine gifts hereafter
shall be brought you for these insults.
Only hold, and do our bidding.'
　　Swift Achilles spoke in answer:
'Your word, goddess, must be taken,
even though the heart be angry.
So 'tis fitting: gods do hearken
unto him that does their bidding.'
So he spoke, and stayed his stout hand
on the great sword's haft of silver,
shut it back inside the scabbard
following Athena's bidding.
She departed to Olympus,
to Zeus' house who bears the aegis,
where the other gods were gathered.
　　Then again the son of Peleus
did berate the son of Atreus,
and his anger was not ended.
'Winebeladen, dog-eyes, deer's-heart!
Never have you had the courage
with the horde to arm for battle,
or to go and wait in ambush
with the bravest of the Achaeans:

that you reckon mortal danger.
Better far to sit surrounded
by the broad Achaean war-host,
and to take away the trophies
of the man that speaks against you.
Fat-fed king, of feeble subjects!
Else these insults, son of Atreus,
were the last that you were making.
Let me tell you this prediction,
swear a mighty oath upon it
by this sceptre, as it never
shall put forth new leaves and branches,
as it now has left its cutting
in the mountains, no more sprouting,
stripped by bronze its bark and leafage—
now the sons of the Achaeans
bear it in their hands for judgment,
they who draw from Zeus their verdicts—
pledge I now my oath upon it.
Time will come when all the Achaeans
will be longing for Achilles.
Then your anguish will not help them,
when in legions they fall dying
at the murdering hands of Hector:
you will rack your heart in anger
that you did allow no honour
to the bravest of the Achaeans.'
These words spoke the son of Peleus,
to the ground he cast the sceptre
gold-bestudded, and was seated.

Wrathful still Atrides faced him.
Then swift rose fair-speeching Nestor,
silvery orator of Pylos;
from his tongue more sweet than honey
ran the words that he could utter.
He had seen two generations
wither of the men born with him,
grown with him in holy Pylos;
o'er the third now he was reigning.
Wishing well he spoke among them:
'O alas, great grief is coming
on the land of the Achaeans.
Priam and the sons of Priam
would rejoice, and all the Trojans
glad in heart would hear these tidings,
how the two of you do quarrel,
who in counsel, who in battle
are supreme among the Danaans.
Hearken to me, I am older,
I have been with men aforetime
finer than the two of you are,
and they never scorned my counsel.
Never more I've seen or shall see
such men living as Pirithous,
Dryas shepherd of his peoples
and Exadius and Caeneus
and the godlike Polyphemus.
Strongest men on earthland grew they,
strongest were, and fought with strongest,
with the centaurs of the mountain,

and most mightily they perished.
Yet with them I was, from Pylos
journeyed far to meet their bidding;
and I fought to my own measure,
but no man could fight against them,
such as men be now on earthland.
Yet did they accept my counsels
and were swayed by my persuasion.
So be you swayed, so 'tis better:
do not thou, though high thy station,
take the maiden from him, leave him
with the prize the Achaeans gave him;
nor do thou, o son of Peleus,
seek to quarrel with the king here.
Never equal are the honours
of a king who holds a sceptre
and from Zeus has exaltation.
Thou art strong, a goddess bore thee:
he is greater, more obey him.
Son of Atreus, quell thy fury,
and I pray Achilles also
leave his wrath, he the great bulwark
in the fray for all Achaeans.'

Answered him lord Agamemnon:
'Aye, all right and proper, old one,
but here is a man desiring
over all to be outstanding,
king of all, of all the master
and commander, which I reckon
will not readily be granted.

If he has been made a spearman
by the gods that are for ever,
must such raillery be therefore
leaping to his lips for utterance?'
   Lord Achilles interrupted:
'Why, a coward faint and feeble
they would call me if I yielded
every business at your bidding.
Unto others give such orders,
not to me, I have no fancy
for obeying you in future.
This too take to heart and ponder:
with these hands I will not fight you
for the girl, nor any other,
as you take away who gave her;
but no more of my possessions
that I have at my black warship
will you take unless I wish it.
Try now, let these men be judges:
soon will black blood spurt on spear.'
   So with hostile words they wrangled,
rose, and ended the assembly
by the ships of the Achaeans.
Peleus' son went to his cabins
and his warships with his followers
and Menoetius' son Patroclus:
Atreus' son a ship gave launching,
and appointed twenty rowers,
and a sacrifice of oxen
put aboard, and fair Chryseis;

and Odysseus the resourceful
went upon it as commander.

    They put forth and sailed the seaways,
while Atrides bade the war-host
do the rites for purifying,
and they purified in order;
in the sea they cast the purgings.
For Apollo made they also
sacrifice of goats and oxen
on the beach beside the breakers,
and the savour up to heaven
all about the smoke went curling.

    With such work the host was busy.
But Atrides kept his quarrel,
kept the threats he made Achilles.
To Eurybates he spoke now
and Talthybius, trusty heralds:
'Go' said he 'unto the cabin
of Achilles, son of Peleus;
take the fair-cheeked girl Briseis
by the hand, and lead her hither.
But if he will not release her,
I myself will come with others,
take her so, and he shall rue it.'
Thus he spoke, with such harsh message
sent them; and they went unwilling
up the beach beside the breakers,
to the Myrmidons' ships and cabins.

    There they found him, by his cabin
and his black ship he was sitting;

and he was not glad to see them.
They in fear and awe before him
stood, before the lord Achilles,
nothing speaking, nothing asking.
But his heart knew, and he hailed them:
'Greetings, heralds, come you hither,
messengers of Zeus and mortals,
for I have no quarrel with you,
only with lord Agamemnon,
who has sent you for the maiden.
Ho, Patroclus, noble scion,
bring Briseis, give her to them;
but be they themselves at witness
unto gods and unto mortals,
and unto that king most haughty,
if hereafter he shall need me
to defend them from destruction.
Baneful now is his heart's raging,
and he knows not how with foresight,
fore˒ and hindsight, both together,
to protect his proud Achaeans
when they fight beside the warships.'

So he spoke; at once Patroclus
turned him to his comrade's bidding,
from the cabin brought Briseis
fair of face, and gave her to them.
Back they went, and she unhappy
with them to the Achaean warships.

Then Achilles left his comrades,
on the grey sea's shore sat weeping,

looking on the boundless water.
Many prayers from there he uttered,
hands outheld to his own mother:
'Mother, as my days are numbered—
so you bore me—the Olympian,
Zeus high-roaring, owes me honour;
yet he does me not the smallest,
for the mighty son of Atreus
has contemned me, and my trophy
taken to his own possession.'

So he spoke amid his weeping,
and his lady mother heard him,
sitting in the salty sea-deeps
in her aged father's dwelling.
Swift she rose from out the grey sea
like a mist, and sat before him
as he wept, her hand caressed him,
and with these words she made answer:
'Child, why weep, what grief assails you?
Tell it, be it shared between us,
in your heart do not conceal it.'
Heavy groaned the swift Achilles:
'But you know, why need I tell you?
We were at Eëtion's township,
holy Thebes, and we did sack it;
all its booty we brought hither,
and it was divided fairly
by the sons of the Achaeans.
For Atrides they selected
one Chryseis, fair-cheeked maiden.

Chryses, priest of lord Apollo,
came then to the Achaean warships
bringing ransom for his daughter,
bringing boundless compensation,
held the wreaths of lord Apollo
on his golden staff, and begged them,
chiefly begged the sons of Atreus,
twin arrayers of the war-horde.
Then the others all consented,
Serve the priest, said the Achaeans,
and accept his compensation.
But Atrides Agamemnon
sent him roughly on his business,
and in harsh words gave him counsel.
Back the old man went in anger,
and Apollo heard his praying,
for he did regard him greatly;
sent his ill shot on the Argives,
and the war-hosts all were dying.
Far and wide the god's compulsion
visited the Achaean army;
and our seer from his true knowledge
told the will of the far-shooter.
I was first to say, Appease him;
but at that the son of Atreus
seized by wrath stood up and uttered
threats, which now have found fulfilment.
For the tendril-eyed Achaeans
bring the girl indeed to Chryse
in a swift ship, bearing offerings

to Apollo the Protector,
but the heralds now have taken
from my cabin Briseus' daughter,
whom I had from the Achaeans.
So, if it be in your power,
grant your son his due protection.
Go implore Zeus on Olympus,
if by any word or action
you have ever done him favour.
Often in my father's palace
I have heard your declaration,
how alone of the immortals
you the black-cloud son of Kronos
rescued from a rude disaster,
when the rest of the Olympians
sought to capture him and bind him,
Hera, Pallas and Poseidon:
how you came and freed him, goddess,
and a hundred-handed helper
summoned quick to great Olympus,
him that gods do call Briareos,
but men everywhere Aegaeon;
for his strength excels his father's.
He then by the son of Kronos
sat in pride of greater prowess,
and the blessed gods did fear him,
and at once gave up their binding.
Now remind him of those doings;
sit by him, his knees embracing
and imploring, if it please him,

that he shall assist the Trojans,
herd the Achaeans by their warships
all along the shore in slaughter,
so that they be all rewarded
on their king's count, and the mighty
lord Atrides see his blindness,
that he did accord no honour
to the bravest of the Achaeans.'

Thetis weeping made him answer:
'Ah, my child! Why did I rear you,
made a mother to misfortune?
By your ships you should be sitting
without grief or lamentation
for the short time that is granted:
now both early death besets you
and unhappiness surpassing.
So ill-fated was my childbed.
But I'll go to snown Olympus,
and your speech I will deliver
unto Zeus whose sport is thunder,
see if he will be persuaded.
You stay sitting by your vessels
with your anger at the Achaeans,
and withdraw from fighting wholly.
Zeus went yesterday to Ocean,
to the virtuous Aethiopians
by the world-encircling river
for to feast, and all the other
gods went with him; on the twelfth day
he will come back to Olympus.

Then to his bronze-treaded mansion
I will go in supplication,
and I think I may persuade him.'
After speaking she departed,
left him there with his heart's ire
rankling for the fair-girt woman
that they took from him unwilling.

   Now Odysseus came to Chryse
with the sacrifice of oxen.
In the harbour deeps arriving
they let down the sails and stowed them
in the black ship, loosened mainstays,
brought the mast down to the mast-box
briskly, rowed her in to moorings,
cast the lodges, tied the stern-ropes.
Out they went above the breakers,
out they brought the gift of oxen
for Apollo, god far-shooting,
out Chryseis went from shipboard.
Then Odysseus the resourceful
brought her to the altar, gave her
to her father, and addressed him:
'Chryses, by lord Agamemnon
I am sent to bring your daughter,
and to sacrifice to Phoebus
tithes of oxen for the Danaans,
so we may appease the great one,
who has sent upon the Argives
grievous woe and lamentation.'
With these words he gave her over

to her father's arms, and Chryses
took his daughter back rejoicing.
  Quickly then they stood the oxen,
holy sacrifice to Phoebus,
lined about the fair-built altar.
Hands were washed, the barley taken
for the casting; and before them
Chryses, hands upheld, made prayer:
'Hear me, god with bow of silver,
lord of Chryse, lord of Killa,
lord of Tenedos and master:
as before you heard my praying,
honoured me, and brought great ruin
to the war-horde of the Achaeans,
so now grant me this wish also:
straightway that same Danaan army
rescue now from rude disaster.'
And Apollo heard his praying.
  So they prayed, and cast the barley.
First they drew the ox's head back,
cut the throat and flayed the carcass,
slit the thighs and wrapped the thighbones
in the fat laid over double,
and raw pieces set upon them.
On the spits the old man burnt them,
and with bronzed wine made libation,
while the younger men, the rowers,
held the five-prong forks beside him.
When the fire had burnt the thighbones
and the inwards had been tasted,

then they carved the other pieces,
stuck them all on skewers, roast them
nice, and drew them off for serving.
When the work was all completed
and the feast was made, they feasted;
and they had the heart for feasting.

When the pangs of thirst and hunger
were dispelled, again the young men
crowned with wine the mixing vessels'
brims, and poured the first cups' measure,
then served everyone in order.
All that day the god with singing
and fair paean they placated,
those young men of the Achaeans,
and with song of the far-shooter;
and it pleased him as he listened.

When the sun was sunk, and darkness
come upon them, then they bedded
where the mooring-ropes were fastened;
but when Dawn appeared, rosefinger
born in mist, they took their sailing
to the broad Achaean war-host;
and Apollo the far-shooter
sent a steady breeze behind them.

Up went mast and white sails spreading,
and the wind blew square to midsail;
all about the keel the dark wave
carolled as the ship went onward,
running seaborne on its journey.
When they reached the Achaean war-host,

onto land they hauled the black ship,
high on shore, and laid the keel-props
all along its length in order;
then dispersed to ships and cabins.

Still in anger by his swift ship
sat the highborn son of Peleus,
never going to assembly
where a man may win distinction,
never going to the fighting.
There with pining heart he rested;
but he felt the want of battle,
and he missed the cries of fighting.

When the dawn came of the twelfth day,
then the gods which are for ever
all together to Olympus
came again, with Zeus before them.
Thetis minded her son's bidding,
and arose from out the sea-swell—
like a mist she was ascending
to high heaven and Olympus;
found the thunderous son of Kronos
sitting parted from the others,
on the highest peak commanding
all the ridges of Olympus.
There she came and sat before him;
by his knees her left hand clasped him,
and below his chin her right hand,
and she spoke in supplication
to the lord Zeus, son of Kronos:
'Father, if by word or action

I have ever done you favour
in the assembly of immortals,
grant this prayer now, and give honour
to my son whose days are numbered
shorter than the other heroes:
for the great lord Agamemnon
has contemned him, and his trophy
taken to his own possession.
You then grant him his due honour,
Zeus, Olympian counsel-maker:
settle victory on the Trojans,
till such time as the Achaeans
honour him and magnify him.'

So she spoke; but Zeus the gatherer
of the stormclouds made no answer,
and for long he sat in silence.
Thetis still his knees was clasping
as before, and clung there firmly,
and a second time she asked him:
'Give me your unfailing promise,
nod your head, or else refuse me—
there can be no fear upon you—
so that I may know how plainly
I rank lowest of the immortals.'

Zeus the gatherer of the stormclouds
answered then with indignation.
'These are now pernicious doings:
you will set me ill with Hera
when she scolds me and provokes me.
Even now she always wrangles

with me in the gods' assembly,
saying that I help the Trojans.
Walk away now, where you came from,
and let Hera notice nothing;
I will make these things my business
to accomplish. Come, I'll grant you
my head's nod, that you may trust me.
This the greatest sign is reckoned
that I give among the immortals:
nothing is deceptive, nothing
taken back, or unaccomplished,
where my head's nod has been granted.'
So he spoke, the son of Kronos,
and his black brows nodded on it.
The ambrosial hair danced upward
from the mighty god's immortal
head; and great Olympus trembled.

    After parleying they parted:
she flew down into the salt deeps
from the brightness of Olympus;
Zeus went in to his own mansion.
All the gods stood up together
from their seats before their father;
no one dared to bide his coming,
and they all stood up before him.
He then on his chair was seated.

    He had been observed by Hera,
and she was aware that Thetis
silverfoot had parleyed with him,
daughter of the sea's old master.

Straight away she started speaking,
scolding Zeus the son of Kronos:
'Which of the immortals this time,
crafty one, has parleyed with you?
You like planning things without me
and deciding things in secret.
You have never chosen freely
to confide your purpose in me.'
    Answered her the son of Kronos,
father both of gods and mortals:
'Hera, do not go expecting
word of all my conversations.
They will be a burden for you,
even though you are my lady.
When it is fit hearing, no one,
god or man, shall know before you;
but when I prefer in absence
from the gods to form my purpose,
do not ask me all these questions.'
    Lady Hera made him answer:
'Son of Kronos, god most fearsome,
how are these your words intended?
Until now 'tis only too true
that I have not asked you questions;
all in quiet you have pondered
what you wanted to consider.
Now I greatly fear that Thetis
silverfoot prevails upon you,
daughter of the sea's old master:
like a mist she sat before you,

clasped your knees in supplication.
I suspect it was for her sake
that you nodded confirmation,
so Achilles shall have honour,
and the Achaeans at their warships
multitudinously perish.'

Answered Zeus the stormcloud-gatherer:
'There's a devil in you—always
you're suspecting and observing.
But you can accomplish nothing;
you will only lose my pleasure,
and it will go harder for you.
If I acted in this fashion,
then that must be how I wish it.
So sit quiet, and obey me,
or the gods may not avail you,
all there are upon Olympus,
when I come and settle with you.'
So he spoke, and lady Hera
was afraid, and sat in silence,
bent aside the heart within her,
and the gods that are from Heaven
were disturbed in Zeus's mansion.

Then Hephaestus, far-famed craftsman,
made to speak to them in service
to his mother, white-armed Hera:
'These will be pernicious doings
that we can support no longer,
if you two make such a quarrel
and for an affair of mortals

set a jackdaw loose among us.
There will be no fun in feasting
what with lower things prevailing.
I advise my mother calmly
(and she knows herself 'tis better)
to do service to our father
Zeus, so he will no more wrangle
and make trouble at our feasting.
What if the Olympian lightner
chooses from our seats to strike us?
He is much the greatest of us.
No, with gentle words address him;
then at once the great Olympian
will be well disposed towards us.'
    With these words he rose up quickly
from his place, a double goblet
handed to his mother, saying:
'Bear it, mother mine, endure it,
or my eyes may see you, dear one,
being struck, and though I sorrow,
nothing then I shall avail you.
Hard to counter is the Olympian.
Once before, when I would help you,
he just seized me by the ankle,
threw me from the wondrous threshold:
all day long I flew, at sunset
down I came to earth in Lemnos;
little heart was left within me.
There by Sintians I was tended.'
White-armed Hera smiled to hear him,

smiling she received the goblet
from her son; and all in order
left to right for all the others
he went pouring out sweet nectar,
dipping from the mixing/vessel.
Unrepressed then rose the laughter
of the blessed gods, beholding
in the halls Hephaestus busy.

They then all day long till sundown
feasted, with the heart for feasting,
for the graceful lyre Apollo
held, and for the Muses' voices
each in turn divinely singing.
When the bright sun passed its setting,
each one to his bed went homeward,
to the house that the illustrious
ambidextrous one, Hephaestus,
by his skill had fashioned for him;
Zeus, Olympian god of lightning,
went to his bed, where he ever
lay when sweet sleep came upon him.
There ascending he sought slumber,
and beside him gold/throned Hera.